griefprints

griefprints

A PRACTICAL GUIDE
FOR SUPPORTING A
GRIEVING PERSON

RADHA STERN

Grief is like fingerprints; everyone grieves in their own way.

Dedicated to my son Christopher,

my sister Michele,

my brothers Adam and Jared

CONTENTS

CONTENTS

Christopher Robin Hotchkiss

May 15, 1974 – March 21, 1996

Introduction

When my son, Christopher, was murdered, I learned the painful way about what any of us can do for a grieving person.

I am no stranger to grief. In addition to my son, I've lost my mother, all four grandparents, two brothers, a sister and dear friends.

After Christopher was murdered, I knew intuitively and immediately that I wanted to live. I have a daughter, a husband and a very close family. So, I very quickly started looking for help with this horrible tragedy.

I have tried many ways to "find comfort." Now, so many years later, I consider myself an expert. I am sharing my journey to help friends and family of those who have lost a dear one. Most of the suggestions I offer are for the early stages of grief. Although no two fingerprints of grief are identical, my hope is that my solace will inspire you to keep looking.

What to Say

No one practices for grieving and trauma.
And in many cases, family and friends of the
grieving person do not know what to say or do
for their loved one who is suffering great loss.

When I am asked, "What can I say?"
I tell people, "Just begin by saying 'hello.'
The words will come."

Josh
Joe
Nan
Kristin
Paul
Brooke
Leah
Michael
Heath
Gideon
Tim
Judah
Rachael
Morris
Ron
Claire
Dave
Annya
Michele
Jessica
Jesse
Rose
Dawn
Sheridon
Robin
Suzy
Gary

Let Them Know You Care

By all means, don't ignore your family/friend/ relative/co-worker who has suffered a loss.

Even if you aren't sure what you should say, know that any recognition of what they are going through will be gratefully received.

The pain of a loss is so intense and raw in the beginning that the person you care for may be out of touch with what you are doing or even saying. But on some level, your presence and caring will register.

I know from experience that everything you do and say is appreciated and significant. Though you may have to wait for an acknowledgement, every expression of caring and concern helps!

When my son, Christopher, was murdered
15 years ago, even if I couldn't express it at
the time, I appreciated every show of support
from family and friends. Whether it was an
arm around my shoulder, a phone call, a card
or a bunch of flowers, I felt people cared
about our family, which comforted me.

What to Do

Naturally, your support and care will differ
with a family member, friend or co-worker.
Above all, do what feels good and right for you.

Too often we underestimate

the power of a touch, a smile,

a kind word, a listening ear,

an honest compliment,

or the smallest act of caring,

all of which have the potential

to turn a life around.

— LEO BUSCAGLIA

Don't Judge

Each of us handles grief in our own time and way. There is certainly no right or wrong way to grieve. Some people stay very active to help themselves cope, while others can't get out of bed. Some people are quiet, while others need to talk. Be gentle in your demands and expectations of the grieving person; this process will take time.

The Long Forever

You left us so quickly,
there were no goodbyes.
How long this forever,
your death and our lives.

The sadness, the anger,
the loneliness of three,
preferring four always,
how small, this new we.

From *Stars in the Deepest Night:*
After the Death of a Child
by Genesse Bourdeau Gentry

Call

Don't worry about what to say; just say, "Hello," and the conversation will unfold. You can take your cues from the person who is grieving. They may tell you how sad or depressed they feel, and you can reply honestly and simply, "Yes, I know how sad you must feel." They may sigh, and all you have to say is, "I cannot even imagine how you feel. I am so sorry and just want you to know if I can do anything at all, I am here for you."

For the first weeks after Christopher was murdered, I was so raw and in so much pain, I felt isolated from the rest of the world. I thought no one could understand what I felt. Just hearing the voice of a friend or a colleague, or simply knowing that they had left a message made me feel less isolated in my grief.

A few of my business friends did not call me when Christopher was murdered. When I saw them months later, I asked them why I hadn't heard from them. They all said, "I wanted to call, but I didn't know what to say." I smiled and told them, "If something like this ever happens again, just call and say, 'Hello.' That's all it takes to offer comfort."

Helping with Phone Calls

One bit of help that relates to phone calls: offer to put a message on the answering machine. At a time like this, calls come in rapidly, and the grieving person doesn't always want to have to answer the phone and talk to people.

The message might say:

> *"Thank you for calling.*
> *Your call is sincerely appreciated.*
> *We will get back to you when we're able."*

You might also answer the phone for part of a day or a portion of each day, making sure to write down who called, and when. That way, the calls are answered, comforting words are received, without putting the grieving person under the stress of performing on demand.

First Phone Call

The first phone call that comes for the person who has passed always takes your breath away. You may want to talk about this, so your loved one or close friend is ready when it happens. Also, you can answer the phone while you are there, if it makes life easier for your person.

Saying Goodbye

It's not in forgetting,
but remembering
that I find peace.

It's not closure,
but opening
that heals my soul.

It's not in letting go,
but holding on
that sets me free.

It's not in saying
goodbye,
but saying hello
that keeps me sane.

Saying hello to the joy,
as well as the pain

hello to the gain,
as well as the loss

hello to the light,
as well as the dark

hello to the good memories,
as well as the bad

hello to the songs,
as well as the silence

hello to her life,
as well as her death —

and never, ever,
saying goodbye.

★

From *Catching the Light:
Coming Back to Life after the Death of a Child*
by Genesse Bourdeau Gentry

Keep Calling

Take it from someone who knows: Do not avoid your friends or family at a time like this.

Your person may need calls for months, even years. Most people call only once. I suggest you "dare to be different" and keep calling. Pick a day of the week.

My sister Kristin stayed with me for a month after Christopher was murdered. Once she went home to Seattle, we began telephoning each other on Mondays (at other times too, but always on Mondays) and we still do. People who hang in with you for the long haul are priceless gifts. Your continued presence will mean the world to your person.

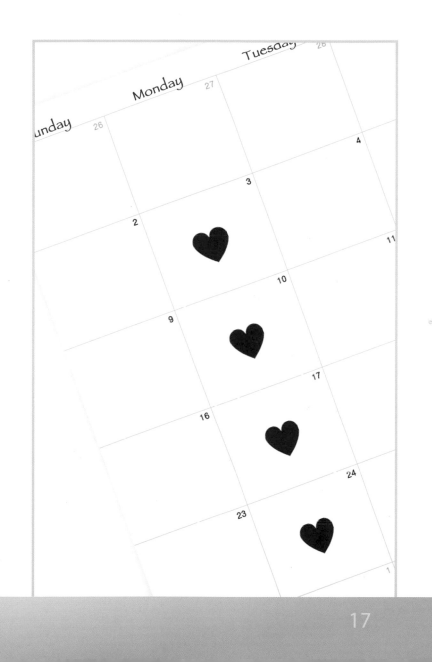

Visit

Your friend, family member or maybe someone you hardly know needs caring for. First, always ask if they are ready for a visit. If they are, check before you visit to see if something is needed. Simple things become very hard when you are in shock from a death.

If you do visit, spend time with the person and allow them to be in whatever shape they are in. When you arrive, ask them what they need at the moment and follow their lead. This might be simply sitting quietly, holding their hand, making a cup of tea, and encouraging them to relax in the garden or take a short walk. Be with them (leave your cell phone in the car).

We did a lot of just sitting after Christopher died. Somehow, the simple presence of other people in the house, not asking anything of me, showing their support for me by their presence, was a comfort.

At this time, it's an effort for the grieving person to get through the day. What you can do best is simply to be there and respond to any needs as they arise.

Errands

Does your family/person need groceries,
dry cleaning picked up, Kleenex (soft kind)
or postage stamps? Are there any phone calls
you can make for them? How about picking
their children up at school? It's important
to help out in small ways, and even more
important to ask first.

It isn't so much the actual doing of the errand
that helps — though of course it does. It's the
offer of contributing to the normal running of
the person's life at such an "unnormal" time.

Talk about the Elephant in the Room

Often people are hesitant to mention the person who has passed. But that is often what the grieving person wants to talk about. If you don't know the grieving person intimately, you might tell them you wish you had known their loved one better. You might ask them to tell you their favorite stories about the loved one who has died. Or you may ask if they would like to show you photographs.

Most people were afraid to mention Christopher, for fear of upsetting me. But this was what I really wanted to talk about. Mentioning Christopher's name, telling stories about him brought him back into the room.

Almost immediately, funny stories about Christopher helped me. My sisters, daughter, brothers and I would sit around and reminisce. "Do you remember when Christopher played Santa Claus and he was so thin he had to put two pillows in his pants?" "Do you remember how he loved lasagna?"

It also helped me to talk about all I had lost with Christopher's murder. I wanted to talk about what the future would and would not offer: no wedding, no more birthdays, and no grandchildren. In losing Christopher, I lost all of that, and I needed to be able to voice these losses and grieve them too.

A freshly grieving person I know has this to say:

"The most meaningful communications I have received are people's fond remembrances of my mom and dad. It's not so much the sweeping generalizations ("what a wonderful person she was"), but rather the specific stories ("I remember this one time when your dad was coaching your little league team…") that I appreciate most. Whether humorous or profound, in the early stages of grief these stories reminded me — in the midst of such overwhelming despair — about how much my parents positively affected other lives. These stories made me feel warm inside at a time when everything seemed unbelievably dark and cold. It was also more meaningful somehow because it was very personal. As far as I'm concerned, it's one of the easier things you can do for a grieving person: simply sharing a story."

Smiling

I could feel you smiling
as I opened the book today.
It felt like, "Good for you, Mom.
This will help you on your way."

I love that small connection,
of knowing that you're there.
It's such a special feeling,
a rainbow I can wear.

★

From *Stars in the Deepest Night:*
After the Death of a Child
by Genesse Bourdeau Gentry

Send Cards

Most people get a flood of cards when they lose their loved one, but the cards quickly stop. Consider sending one card a week for a while. Very small gestures of kindness go a long way. If you wonder what to write in a card or a series of cards, consider searching for thoughtful quotations you consider appropriate. Copy a favorite poem. Or paste in a lovely image. Some messages you might write:

> *"May your days become easier and may you be comforted by friends, family and happy memories."*

> *"I don't know what I could say to help you. I just know I must write to you and say how sorry I am. I am thinking of you and want to express my sincerest sympathy."*

> *"I'm remembering what an amazing person your (husband, child, wife, father, mother) was. I will always think of (your person) when I see magnolia blossoms. I know he/she loved magnolias."*

> *"What do we live for*
> *if not to make life less*
> *difficult for each other?"*
>
> GEORGE ELIOT

Many years ago dear friends Karl and Tony went to Boston for an experimental cancer treatment. I sent them off with a personal "Get Well" card to open every day for Karl. I called the packet my "one-a-day multiple vitamins." My husband, Gary, and I wrote jokes, silly quotes and "don't forget to be nice to the nurses" on the cards. When I talked to these friends on the telephone, Tony said that he and Karl both brightened up every day when it was time for Karl to open his card.

Bring Flowers

Grief is a hard way to get flowers, but their beauty does help. If you bring flowers, it's helpful to arrange them in a vase ahead of time. If you bring loose flowers, arrange the flowers in one of the household vases when you arrive.

Dealing with flowers can be overwhelming in early stages of grief, so you might also consider a potted plant, which doesn't require a vase and lasts much longer than cut flowers.

Be mindful of allergies. If you have the time during your visit, it is often helpful to tend to the flowers that have already arrived.

My sister Kristin was the flower queen.
She would wake up early every day at my house
and tend to all the flowers sent by family and friends.
We saved all the rose petals from bouquets I received
and dried them for Christopher's resting place.
I have always loved dried flowers, and collecting
the rose petals was a way to include everyone.

I still save rose petals from special occasions —
dinner with friends, a wedding shower or ceremony,
a baby shower or flowers sent by loved ones. I take
these petals to where we scattered Christopher's ashes
so I can share the experience with him.

Offer Small Treats
to the Family

Everyone needs to eat. Do your best to offer healthy, nutritious food. If your person/family has a craving for something, bring it. Treats in life are important and comfort is hard to find for the newly grieving. Remember to inquire about dietary restrictions.

Cook a Nutritious Meal

Make food and bring it, or cook for the grieving person or family in their home.

When someone receives a meal you have prepared for them, they feel cared for. And at the same time, you feel that you have contributed something toward their sustenance at such a difficult time.

Again, ask about dietary restrictions. As well, you might ask if they need the food. Too much of a good thing can become a burden at this difficult time. If they would like a meal, you might also ask whether they would like you to eat with them, or simply to drop the meal discreetly off at their front door.

Right after Christopher was murdered our next door neighbor brought us barbecued chicken they had prepared on their grill, along with a salad and cookies. Somebody else brought over a brisket, prepared from her mother's delicious recipe. We loved the hearty food offered to us, though others may prefer lighter meals when they are in grief.

I love to make soup, and believe soup made with love helps. Some of the soups I make are: chicken soup, to which I often add vegetables; tomato bisque; white bean with sausage soup; and lentil soup (see page 35). I enjoy the chopping and the brewing of all the flavors when I make soup, and I know it's healthy. If you have something special you love to cook, make that for your person. People love receiving pasta sauce, meatloaf, macaroni and cheese, quiche — any food that can be kept on hand or that freezes well. And knowing it's one of your favorites makes it more special.

More about Food

Cook a meal together of the deceased's favorite food. Our family still celebrates Christopher's birthday with his favorite food, or we go to Benihana, his favorite restaurant. This can be a wonderful time for your person. A kitchen with loved ones can be a very healing place.

Lentil, Split Pea and Bean Soups – Basic Recipe

1 medium onion (I prefer sweet), chopped
4 carrots, cleaned and chopped
5 celery stalks, cleaned and chopped
1 large can diced tomatoes in juice
    (NOT FOR SPLIT PEA!)
Salt / Pepper
Ham steak / pork sausage (optional)
2 cups lentils / beans / split peas (whichever you prefer),
    rinsed thoroughly
Water

onion, carrots, celery and legume of choice
peas) in a soup pot — and cover with
until things are soft.
Chec   add more liquid.

2917

If you are using toma   he end of
cooking (they are not recom   ). You can
also add some tomato puree if you li   omato flavor.

For lentil and split pea, I add cubed ham steak. For bean
soups, I cook pork sausage / Italian sweet sausage / spicy
chorizo and add the cooked meat (with juices for added
flavor) at the same time as the tomatoes.

IF YOUR SOUP STICKS, DO NOT STIR IT!!!
Pour it into another clean pot and keep going.

Run Small Errands

Small errands become difficult. Help however you can. Ask for a grocery list — please don't just guess. Going to public places is very hard in the beginning. The person who is grieving feels so exposed and vulnerable. Picking up groceries for a grieving person or family means both that they don't have to force themselves into a public place and that there is one less thing to take care of.

Offer to go to the post office, the drug store to pick up sundries, even the hardware store. There may be library books that need to be returned or bills that need to be paid. Put yourself in the grieving person's place and imagine what you might need. Your person may wish to accompany you. It can be comforting to do normal things, but having you there and doing the driving adds a sense of security.

After Christopher was murdered, I had a hard time going out in public, even to the grocery store or post office. I felt so vulnerable because I was in so much pain. If I needed to go somewhere where there were a lot of people, I would take Gary or a friend. I could cry at any moment and I wanted someone near who understood me. It is also hard to observe other people whose lives are going along without any apparent trauma when yours is filled with it.

Send Emails
(once you've contacted the person)

If your grieving person communicates by email, email them. Just a quick note to let them know you are thinking about them. "I'm here when you need me." "I hope there's a little sunshine in your day somewhere." They may not answer at first, but when they do look at their email, they will REALLY appreciate you thinking of them. For somebody fresh with grief, nothing feels normal. An added benefit of a quick email is that it takes them back to a time when life was intact, and that can feel good, if only for a moment.

Remember that you can also send cards, images and photos via email. Some people need a bit of time before you send photos. Photos can make a person very sad in the beginning, but at the right time, they all become so very precious.

Remember the Children

Children can be overlooked when grieving
is fresh and life becomes chaotic. Include
the children in whatever you do. And don't
underestimate what they understand.
Sometimes protecting children is harmful.
Let them participate in appropriate ways.
At the funeral/memorial, for example, the
children can read a poem, scatter rose petals,
light a candle or tell a story.

Send a sympathy card to the child/children too.
Ask them "How are you doing with all this?"

If needed, advise school counselors about
the family situation. Do something with the
children by themselves so they feel your love
and caring. This helps the adults too.

I took my daughter, Christina, to the grieving group (The Compassionate Friends) I joined. What she needed was not always what I needed but we were together. Our grieving paths are very different. She lost her brother and best friend, while I lost my son. One of the hardest parts of Christopher's death for me was seeing my daughter in so much pain.

Four years after Christopher's murder, when our oldest grandchildren were seven and ten, their father died. In addition to everything we did, soon after the death, Gary and I picked the kids up and took them to dinner. Shortly after this, we created "Family Night" for the extended family. We have continued the tradition. Every other Sunday, all of us get together for dinner. We rotate who cooks, and if it's your birthday, you can choose the menu. It is a wonderful tradition that really makes us all feel connected.

Ask Questions

Such as:

"How are you doing since the death of
_____?"

"How are you managing since the death of
_____?"

"Are you getting what you need
to get through this?"

"Are you taking care of yourself?"

"Are there any questions you have,
or anything you want to talk about?"

These are very caring questions
which few people ask.

I remember that despite my grief over losing Christopher, I often felt I had to take care of other people. The situation was too awful for them to think about. So when someone wanted to know how I really felt, it was a relief knowing that I didn't have to take care of them.

Normally, when people asked, "How are you?" I would answer, "Fine." But when I heard the words, "How are you really? How are you dealing with missing Christopher and his death?" I was always grateful. Instead of automatically answering, "I'm fine," I could respond fully, "This really is a nightmare. I miss Christopher and it's unimaginable that he's not coming back."

Ask about Specifics

You might also ask the grieving person if they are having difficulty with any part of their life, including sleeping and eating.

Often, the grieving person will have great difficulty sleeping initially. You might ask your friend, relative, co-worker about their sleep, and if they are having difficulty, you might offer them a relaxation CD to listen to at night, or natural sleeping aids — before they go to prescription.

If they have no appetite, you may explore with them what far-fetched dish might just appeal to them. I have a friend who offers milkshakes to her friends in mourning, and the friends respond quite positively to a treat that takes them back to a time before their loss.

Empty Places

I drove the old way yesterday.
It'd been a while, you see.
And there, without a warning,
the pain washed over me.

I drove the old way yesterday
and sadness came on strong,
taken back by so much feeling,
since you've been gone so long.

Places seem to lie in wait
to summon up the tears,
to say remember yesterday,
those days when you were here.

Places where you laughed and played
are places where I cry.
These places held the memories
that will live as long as I.

★

From *Stars in the Deepest Night:*
After the Death of a Child
by Genesse Bourdeau Gentry

Be Gentle with Opinions

This one is BIG. A natural death at a very old age is different from a death due to crime. If your grandfather died at 99 years old and the person you are speaking with has a son or daughter who has died, please do not say, "I know how you feel." These two losses are very different experiences. It is out of the natural order to outlive your child, and for the rest of your life, you will miss the child who is no longer with you.

My "mother on earth" (my mother passed when I was only 19, so Beth Burstein and I adopted each other) came to the house the day Christopher was murdered and said, "Don't let anyone tell you that you need to get over this. You never have to get over this." I was so relieved that people did not expect me to "get over" the death of my son. All I wanted was one day to pass his picture without shedding a thousand tears.

Don't Try to Fix
Your Person/Family

People grieve; it should be a process. And the process is different for each one of us. Be gentle with your judgments of how you think the grief should be. Some people are private about their grief, some are public, so don't push the expression of grief. My mother used to say, "Everything will dovetail." What she meant was that in its own time, this will work out. This is the way of grief. For each of us it unfolds in a different way.

Some people need to stay very busy. Some people need to stay at home. Their new life/world is so overwhelming and painful, it is even hard to get out of bed. People need time for the healing process. It is not something you can rush.

I realized almost instantly after Christopher was murdered that I wanted to live through all this pain. I went one step more and declared that, "I not only want to live but thrive." I felt beyond any reasonable doubt that Christopher would not want me to be miserable down here. I wanted to honor who he was and live a more significant life because of his murder. That all being said, it was not easy. I felt so distraught; it was difficult to know what to do sometimes, particularly in the very beginning of this journey. Who practices for this kind of experience? I felt like I was going where no man/woman had gone before.

I gave myself permission to take it one hour and then one day at a time.

Help Care for Family Pets

Many grieving people need to travel and attend to family matters. Also, they may not have the energy to take care of any person or animal. When you are deeply hurting, every little thing is a huge effort. Yet the grieving person still cares deeply about their pet/s.

Some things you can do:

> Walk the dog
> Take the dog to the groomer
> Buy pet food and supplies
> Change the litter box

You might even offer to take the cat/dog home with you for a short time to relieve the family of responsibility. Animal care can be short term or long term. Just ask if you can help.

Someone I know took over walking her friend's dog after her friend died. At the memorial her friend's parents mentioned how much that simple act had meant to them.

> *No act of kindness, no matter how small, is ever wasted.*
>
> — AESOP (620 BC - 560 BC)

Clean the Person's House

Cleaning their house is the last thing on a grieving person's mind. Offer to clean their house. Put on music, go about the cleaning with gusto, and have the person in mourning relax. You can also hire a service to come in. Life takes a lot of maintenance; when your life has changed so quickly and you are grieving, it is very hard to keep up. Things can start to unravel quickly if not taken care of.

You can help the grieving person maintain their home in one of these ways:

Tidy up the kitchen, wash dishes, etc.

Check the refrigerator for food gone bad

Make the beds

Help with gardening

Water and care for inside plants

Pick up their mail

Help with bills, correspondence and thank you notes for flowers

Do a load of laundry

Take dry cleaning in

You might even offer to do small household repairs, if needed.

Offer Small Opportunities for Self Care

Offer your person a massage. Massage can be very grounding; it can help the grieving person relax and let go of all the tension and stress around the death of their loved one.

Once your person feels they can venture outside the home, you might suggest going for a manicure or pedicure, a hair appointment. Often simply getting out of the house for a short time without having to socialize is a welcome relief, a brief taste of normalcy.

After Christopher was murdered, I didn't know
where my body ended and where the world began.
So much had shifted. I used to go outside and feel
the cold on my skin because I was not sure who I was
or what I was feeling in the beginning. Everything
was so unreal and I felt very out of touch. Massage
brought me back into my body and into the world,
giving me a more solid foundation on which to rebuild
my life. I found massages a very safe place to cry,
and simply told the therapist, "If I cry, don't worry."

Remember HUMOR
Is a Great Healing Tool

Don't be afraid to say anything funny. At such a time, people crave what feels normal, and for most of us, laughter is an important part of life.

Be mindful. If the laughter comes out of something spontaneous in the middle of loving words, that is wonderful. But trying to make them laugh for laughter's sake would probably backfire with anyone who is newly bereaved.

The first time I laughed was a big moment.
I did not know if I would ever laugh again.

I can't honestly remember what made me laugh the
first time, but it was a genuine laugh from the belly.
I noticed it (I remember this) and was pleased.
It felt like a small positive step.

Understand That the "First" of Everything Is Hard

The first of everything is the worst when you are deep in grief: the first hour, the first day, the first week, the first month, and the first year. Friends and family can be aware of all these firsts and how difficult they are for the grieving person. Acknowledging these difficult times and thinking of small ways to support the person can be a comfort.

Christopher was killed on a Thursday morning (March 21, 1996) and I dreaded Thursday mornings for a long time. If you are aware of the day on which the person died, you might simply phone your friend or family member and leave a message letting them know you are thinking of them.

Possessions

Another very hard first is going through the loved one's possessions. Your support can help in many ways. There are so many reminders with personal possessions. Just your being there will make all the difference. Offer to help send things to other family members, make a Goodwill trip for them and pack carefully possessions that they want to keep for now. Some people never get rid of their loved one's things, or keep them for years before doing something with them. This is okay too!

Other Difficult Firsts

- Anniversaries — birth, death and wedding

- Birthdays

- Holidays

- Vacations

- Eating at a favorite restaurant

- Cooking the loved one's favorite foods

- Going to bed without their spouse

- Going to the loved one's special places

- Visiting with friends, colleagues, family of their loved one

- Attending the first social event

- Attending cultural events — movies, sports, concerts — they used to attend with their loved one

All endings are also beginnings.

We just don't know it at the time.

— MITCH ALBOM

Obituary and Memorial

Writing the obituary can be an overwhelming task. If you are able to help write the obituary, this can be an intimate experience and a real gift.

Offer to help with the memorial. There are so many decisions to make and your person will be in a state of shock. Gently make suggestions, help coordinate the food, buy a lovely blank book for people to leave a message.

Death is nothing at all. It does not count. I have only slipped away into the next room. Nothing has happened. Everything remains exactly as it was. I am I, and you are you, and the old life that we lived so fondly together is untouched, unchanged. Whatever we were to each other, that we are still. Call me by the old familiar name. Speak of me in the easy way which you always used. Put no difference into your tone. Wear no forced air of solemnity or sorrow. Laugh as we always laughed at the little jokes that we enjoyed together. Play, smile, think of me, pray for me. Let my name be ever the household word that it always was. Let it be spoken without an effort, without the ghost of a shadow upon it. Life means all that it ever meant. It is the same as it ever was. There is absolute and unbroken continuity. What is this death but a negligible accident? Why should I be out of mind because I am out of sight? I am but waiting for you, for an interval, somewhere very near, just round the corner. All is well. Nothing is hurt; nothing is lost. One brief moment and all will be as it was before. How we shall laugh at the trouble of parting when we meet again!

Excerpt from May 1910 sermon
by Canon Henry Scott Holland (1847–1918)
Canon of St. Paul's Cathedral, London

Mail

Some grieving people have a hard time dealing with the mail of the person who has passed. Some of the mail will be important and must be looked at, while other mail will be requests for funds or advertisements for sales. You can help go through the letters with your person. If the sender needs to be informed, you might be able to help with that. Mail is very personal; so keep this in mind as you are helping.

*If you're looking for a way to help a grieving person,
dealing with unwanted mail could be it — especially if
they are not computer savvy and you are, even a little.*

*The United States Postal Service provides a website,
"Manage Mail for the Deceased."*

*It briefly tells you just what to do: change of address
or forward, if needed. You can do everything online.*

*To cancel all future mailings, they direct you to the
Direct Marketing Association's "Deceased — Do Not
Contact" list. Register the deceased and mailings
should stop within three months.*

*This may seem like a little thing, but it helps the
person, the household, and the environment —
and everybody feels better.*

Photos

Help make a photo album. It may take some time for your person to be able to look at pictures without crying. Every picture becomes a treasure when a loved one passes. Help them sort through the piles and scan them or make an album.

Photo: Charlie Weinstein

Listen and Write

Ask the grieving person to tell you memories and stories, both sad and funny. Write them down, then give them to the person at the appropriate time, either immediately or later when they are ready.

When Christopher was sixteen, we went on vacation with his best friend Mike's family, to Portland, Oregon. One day the boys all went out in a boat, onto Lake Oswego, to go fishing. Nobody caught anything, and the junior fishermen were so disappointed, they stopped at a fish market on the way home to buy a fish! I still treasure the "proud" photo of Christopher I snapped when they got home.

Comforting Distractions

Give soothing music, as well as feel-good movies, books on grief and sweet stories that your person can disappear into. Your person may not be ready for these; however, they will be there when they are. It took me a long while to get to the point I was ready to read. Music soothed me from the beginning. I still have special "Christopher" songs, which include Bob Marley's "No Woman, No Cry" and its refrain, "Everything's going to be alright" and Natalie Cole singing her father's song "Autumn Leaves" (*I miss you most of all, when Autumn leaves start to fall…*).

*Every experience deeply
felt in life needs to be passed
along. Whether it be through
words and music, chiseled in stone,
painted with a brush, or sewn with
a needle, it is a way of reaching
for immortality.*

— THOMAS JEFFERSON

Garden

Work alongside the grieving person in their garden. Gardening is a very healing activity. Even watching you work in the garden can soothe a person in mourning. Plant a special tree or plant for the person who has passed. We have some very lovely trees in our garden for Christopher, which are now quite tall.
I also planted the plants people gave us at the memorial, and when they bloom I smile.

Other Kind Gestures

Whatever your heart may suggest will most likely be right. Don't tiptoe around or walk on eggshells. Be yourself, the person they know.

I've offered many suggestions, but in the end, caring for someone going through the grieving process is intuitive. When you are involved with someone and see their life and their grief, what you can do to help will often occur to you. Remember, however, to be sensitive to your person's wants and needs; it is not always what you think they need. Usually, listening to what you feel and following your heart will lead you in the right direction.

And remember, through all this: don't forget your own self-care. You can't take on the stresses of another person if you are depleted yourself.

I'm swinging into your heart!
Chris

Grief comes to you all at once,
so you think it will be over all at once.
But it is your guest for a lifetime.

How should I treat this guest?
This unwelcome, uninvited guest.

Think of the one who sent it to you…

From *Kayak Morning*
by Roger Rosenblatt

Thank you...

The writing took a small village.

I would like to thank my family for all their love, blessings and support.

Extra special thanks goes to my brother, Paul, who has always been there for me.

Also, deep thanks to my compassionate friends Georgia Alioto, Genesse Gentry, David Rosenthal, Lisa Klairmont, Jessalyn Nash, Stacey Redman, Julia ODaly and Jaimee Karroll, who gave me suggestions and help along the way.

I was pushed into writing by my friend Lorie Rice. She deserves a special thank you.

Thanks to my writing teachers —
Adair Lara, Jon Carroll and Isabel Allende.

And Jane Anne Staw, my writing coach,
who is simply the best.

Thanks to Mark Burstein, for his final copyediting.

The quilt (shown in full on page 82) was made by
Liz Piatt to whom I will always be grateful. Thank you.

The quilt photography was done by my brother,
Zalman Stern. Thank you.

Thanks to Gary Maxworthy (my darling husband)
for photography (rose petals, cover painting, author).

The wonderful design was done by Lory Poulson.
Thank you.

And to Karen Peterson (whose art is on page 84) —
thank you for so many things!

Finally, thanks to Malcolm Margolin and Diane Lee
of Heyday, a community treasure.

About the Author

Since the murder of her son, Christopher, in 1996, Radha Stern has devoted herself to helping others who have lost a loved one due to a violent crime, for whom she maintains the website Griefprints.com. She is active in Law Center to Prevent Gun Violence and the Insight Prison Project, as well as The Compassionate Friends, an organization for parents who have lost a child. Radha is an experienced grant maker, fundraiser, and marketer, and her extensive volunteer activity over the last two decades includes work with trade organizations, advocacy groups, and victim's rights programs. She is a past member of the Board of Directors for the Tenderloin Neighborhood Development Corporation; program officer for a family philanthropic foundation that supports organizations providing basic services to critical-need populations, and a volunteer at the San Francisco and Marin Food Banks. Radha is a contributor to the inspirational book *Courage Does Not Always Roar: Ordinary Women with Extraordinary Courage* (Simple Truths, 2010). A native Californian, she lives with her husband, Gary; together they have five children and five grandchildren.

The liberating power of grief

THE COMPASSIONATE FRIENDS

To all parents who are looking for help, I would
suggest The Compassionate Friends, an amazing
organization that helped me from week one.
All these years later I still keep in touch.

*"The Compassionate Friends is about transforming the
pain of grief into the elixir of hope. It takes people out of the
isolation society imposes on the bereaved and lets them
express their grief naturally. With the shedding of tears,
healing comes. And the newly bereaved get to see people
who have survived and are learning to live and love again."*

— Simon Stephens, founder, The Compassionate Friends

National website:
www.compassionatefriends.org

(The chapter locater is under Find Support
on the home page of the website.)

A Wise and Practical Gift from the Center of Grief. No one knows what to say. No one knows what to do. But we do and say I hear, we are here. A wise book of practical details, survival details. You don't get over grief, but it shapes you, and the new shape includes you.

Richard Baker/Zentatsu

Radha's book is a jewel of comfort for grieving hearts. Through empathy and visual beauty she manages to reach into the places where people have experienced hurt and grief with a healing touch.

Rabbi Zalman Schachter-Shalomi, *From Age-ing to Sage-ing*

At one time or another, we are all faced with the need to comfort and support a grieving person, but more often than not, we feel inadequate and awkward. Drawing from her own experience, and a deep vein of wisdom and commonsense, Radha Stern provides practical, and truly meaningful advice for all of us.

Deborah Hopkinson, children's author

Gorgeous. This sweet, smart, sensible book is both a visual and heart-felt gem. The perfect safety net for that black hole of grief that few of us are ever prepared for.

Chip Conley, founder of Joie de Vivre Hotels and author

When a loved one or friend suffers a loss of someone dear to them, we don't know how to respond. We want to help, but don't want to intrude. This book is a gift as it gently guides us to help the people we love through what may be the hardest time they'll ever face. It's a book of compassion and a book of love.

David Sheff, author of *Beautiful Boy: A Father's Journey through His Son's Addiction* and *Clean: Overcoming Addiction and Ending America's Greatest Tragedy*

Radha has written a most touching and personal account of her emotional struggle after the murder death of her beautiful son Christopher. This account will serve as an inspiration to others on the same painful journey and those wanting to help. The honest sharing of the aftermath of Christopher's violent death gives insight and hope to all. I commend Radha for reaching outside her pain to help others. She is an inspiration to us all.

Carol Kearns, Ph.D., author of *Sugar Cookies and a Nightmare*

It is a rare person who can offer meaningful advice to those suffering the loss of a loved one and to those wanting to console them. Radha Stern, forged by the tragedy of the murder of her own child, has emerged from that cauldron to offer us Griefprints. She has surpassed her goal of providing a practical guide for grieving. Her wisdom is presented with such extraordinary beauty and grace that she has also given us a guide for praising the gift of life.

Harvey Gould, author of *A Fierce Local –
Memoirs of My Love Affair with Ireland*

Death is cold, cruel. In a split second, it's too late to turn back the clock. For survivors, everything is hard. Even breathing can seem an impossible task. What do you say to a person in grief who has lost a loved one? Are there words? Are there simple acts that can ease the pain? In her tender, beautiful book, Radha Stern, a survivor of her own dark grief, shows us the way to care for ourselves and each other when we are lost and don't know how.

Nancy Mullane, author of *Life After Murder:
Five Men in Search of Redemption*

For further information,
please visit Radha Stern's website,
Griefprints.com